NINE SERIES

Pushed Toward the Blue Hour

Tracy Gaughan
Claire Loader
K.T. Slattery

Published by Nine Pens
2022
www.ninepens.co.uk

All rights reserved: no part of this book may be reproduced without the publisher's permission.

The right of the author to be identified as the author of this work has been asserted by them in accordance with the Copyright, Designs and Patents act 1988

ISBN: 978-1-7398274-3-4

NS 004

Tracy Gaughan
- 7 Noli me tangere
- 9 Girl of the Seine
- 11 Capture
- 12 On the Elf Hill
- 13 Daylight Saving
- 14 Blue
- 15 Auguries
- 18 to never know
- 20 Jacob's Ladder

Claire Loader
- 25 There are Days
- 26 Standstill
- 27 Nebulous
- 28 Telling the Bees
- 29 Fallow
- 30 The School Gate
- 31 Utility
- 32 Monochrome
- 33 Winter's Fruit

K.T. Slattery
- 37 I Am
- 38 If, When, How
- 39 Escape to 1984
- 40 10th of December 2020
- 41 October Daisy
- 42 Immigrant
- 43 On the Eve of the Eve of my 39th Birthday
- 44 The Serenity Prayer Word Jumble
- 46 Between the Last Bell of Summer and the First Bell of Fall

Tracy Gaughan

Writer, editor and broadcaster, Tracy Gaughan lives in Galway. A finalist in the 2021 Jacar Press Eavan Boland Award, her work has appeared in Crannóg, Headstuff, Boyne Berries, Live Encounters and elsewhere. She holds an MA in International Literatures from NUIG and is IRL/UK poetry editor at the Blue Nib Literary Magazine.

Noli me tangere

I'll never get to feel like that feather
lying in the air inside a chicken coop
after a massacre, if you don't touch me

like the moon on a naked tree in some
mist on glass, frost in grass, post-resurrection
encounter in a garden at midnight.

Don't touch me like a satin cloth spread out
on a table. No oak apple ink soaking
pelt or skin or paper. Don't skin me

like a fish fin breaking surface in a V,
unzipping clothes that fall away, as
melodies in dreams. Fingers slipping

under seams and sliding to one side,
a locksmith with a key fitting wards
like a sheet to an un-dressed bed.

My leg is a flag around a mast.
Don't touch me in the littoral, roiling sea
leaves me amorous for your mouth

for skin of your teeth. Don't tickle my metrical feet
with your tongue, don't singe me with your sun
or rouse that helpless singing bowl, O -

don't touch me with my own helplessness
or take yes for an answer; don't take it,
that flat blade to a pomegranate. No

bracelet to the wrist, don't do it, that fern
in an autumn shiver and tambourine tingle.
That luthier tuning pegs on a violin

when there's nothing wrong. Don't muscle me
over the birch block knee, don't touch me
please, with that leather halter throat-latched to a horse.

Girl of the Seine

Resusci Annie was modelled on the death mask of an unknown girl-
L'inconnue de la Seine - who drowned in Paris, c. 1880

When I heard the toymaker, Asmund, loved you
I thought it was a love story. But when I asked:
are you okay? caressed your head, I saw you wore
the face of the dead. Parisian pleasure girl, they said

murdered herself; an unfortunate child who drank the Seine.
Whose legend are you, inconnue? Hoofed or winged?
No matter. Beautiful suicide sank to the grave,
fished out in nets of Saint-Cloud. Annie resusci,

sans soucis, sans merci, a fallen woman bitter as gall
who needed to be dead to be loved. When the water
drowned your stains they worshipped you, a heroine.
That mute smile of salvation was a souvenir cast

a thousand times, a coveted *objet d'art*. L'inconnue,
you grew neither young nor old but numerous.
The poets and mourning lovers who put death
safely in you, inscribed your face with fantasy,

and necrophilic lusts, ill-used you as Asmund, who
knew those lips, well versed in kisses could save
a life. I compress your chest, sweet Annie resusci,
sans soucis, sans merci. You are death by proxy,

pleasing to those who stilled your sacred harp
that foggy night; tiny boots running twixt lamppost
and linden, a ghost on the banks of the Seine. My
mouth on your mouth, I can't breathe their want

into you, Annie: erotic corpse, Nabokov's itch,
inanimate woman. I come to your river, close your
button nose, hold your mouth shut tight
like an oyster and let you go.

Capture

The man in front's neck is my grandfather's.
        Its rifts and corrugations a web of fields
        in Mayo. His heavy breath an ebb of water,
        harsh in stripping-winds that knew those hayrick
        hands, their silk-stained, poitin-making, salmon-
        fishing toil. Memories of him live on the pulse
        like birds on the wing. He's coming *con brio*
        to the windowsill, my mother driving him home
        after pints and fisticuffs. I'm in the back seat,
        frightened by talk of will-o'-the-wisp dangling
        his haunt across lowland bogs, marsh flowers
        in flush all the way to the coast. Crunching gravel
        alerts a dog dozing by emerald-green mossy banks,
        nearby he's scything scutch-grass stalks and nettles.
        He's handing me Hazel to herd the cattle home
        for milking - strange stalactites softening in my hands,
        in his hands that bring me tea in bed in a china cup.
        I'm a queen feeding gold to scratching chickens,
        a wild compass, swinging from oakwood beams
        in the hayloft. I remember a tip-toe of moonlight
        on frosty blue tiles, listening to the house inhale
        through an open window, noise of night's whickering
        badgers and hooting owls, the sleepy Atlantic tonguing
        an archipelago of rocks, buoys, an upturned pail mourning
        the death of something loveable far away. I can see him
        booted in perseverance, shoring his curragh on some
        unfrequented beach off the sound. Then, simply standing
        there, trying to catch an abstract moment of light
        before being ambushed by sea ...
by the man in front's neck.

On the Elf Hill
    after Harry Clarke

They gather up their trains of silk and come to tread a measure
On the hill. The faces of girls, and stones about all wet
With moonshine. A shred of song in hissing Ash they dance
Between flower and star in gracefully woven scarves of mist.
Their innocence light, moth feet on skin. The boys drinking

To brotherhood, backs pressed up to stone-cold walls watching
The girls spin, round and round in silver-gold flames of fire.
They fall like motes in sudden cockcrow terrain, polished
With butter, with innocent virgin light. One boy wraps his coat
About a girl and carries her away. Light as a feather.
Weightless as a dream.

Daylight Saving

    Falling back, you think of those ancestors who went to bed
in barley-gold and rose to light-pared winter and raw-structure.
If they hadn't lost the hour, would they have seen it coming:
the opposite of meaning, the otherness, the theft of a mother
tongue that none could utter. The upside downness
    of trees, kicking their roots in the air. Crows hungrier
than wolves. Ferns dyeing and dying in summer-quiet rivers
already bugling over banks and swallowing rutted swards;
rushing to remember things before the boning, before
lush leaves lost faith and hedgerows receded like old gums.
They were generation Vulnerable, as new clay, or autumn-wheat
toupee on ploughed up soil.
    Words dress thoughts like overcoats, and they wondered
why nothing they said ever fit. Why the language of their hearts
clotted in their mouths and winter contrived her own cold colours
against them. They were mute oaks in the greenwood, rows
of disfigured Daphnes proudly waiting for their voices to be heard
above the painful saw and sever.
    Twice a year you switch forward and back, you lose, you gain
at dawn and dusk. Come spring, you'll walk the forest path, search
for things lost in the forward hour and you'll feel it, like a phantom
limb: the burning pain of loss that lives on, the itch, the pins and
needles.
    All that activity at the stumps.

Blue

When I was fighting hard to love   the lake was blue
and what your baldness offered in umber   floundered
in all the Kleinness   the expansive dimensionless blue
that sirened me in Gagarin style.   Sirened me in
like a hope   that reigns a king a while then dies.
Your blue for me was not the blue of blue depths.
It was sad   and bald   and Picasso-y.
It was a hard-cold frost-stiff   foot in the face.
I was no monarchist fighting for love.   I was losing it
carelessly   the way a child loses a glove in a meadow.
Give me mud   the muddy brown filthiness of rivers,
tannin-rich   silt-laden grime that never accuses as blue does.

See how blue's authority stains the skin: Tuaregs, Krishna
Madonna's robe and its verdict.
You were swimming away in nakedness, bobbing in the dumb   blue
womb of a lake   the bank wrapped around you.
I was verb mother, like the wolf and boy, feeding marsh-rats

and quail to a face   between my legs.
A bitch in a forest of birches   looking up at a sky I despised
for its blueness.
Blue earth.   Pale blue dot of how little we matter.
How we matter little   to one another.

Auguries

Anglepoise on the shelving margin of an ink-black river, I wait motionless for a meal to come. Trespassing streetlights whet carp and minnow, ensnaring them in shallow pools beneath. A mongrel behowls a shadow. Nearby, a harvest mouse climbs the grass,

makes her way home. I strike. Bayoneted, my prey abandons hope. I'm not the only hunter. A vixen prowls. Last night her hunger took five. Siphoned the innocent embryos straight out of their calcified houses; the swans are hysterical, still. I leave them

treading jagged shells of grief and take flight, navigating the edifices of this great city: her rooflines and steeples, watchtowers, and arches. The glistening stars and gibbous moon plot my path; presage my arrival. A portentous bird, I pause on a rough-cast plinth outside a hospital window.

To some behind it, I'm a stork, to others a scythe. To the woman outstaring, I'm a vision, an assumpting Madonna, veil-billowing a narcotic nocturne. Yesterday, her excised breast left the operating room. Now she sees it everywhere: a child's bobble cap, a cathedral's cupola.

Bars expectorate. A congregational din breaks our accord and I take flight. Down-stream atop a bridge, a young man contemplates the riverbed. Like a gannet, he plunges. Boots and all. He doesn't know it, but it will be two months before he resurfaces. Peripherally, something lies abandoned in a doorway. Leg-splayed like a vivisected frog is a violated woman. Hell is empty. I take flight. This city disconcerts me. Sometimes it's a poet's dream, sometimes a viper's nest, a sewer. An abrading cart is being pushed toward the blue hour by a garbageman: a man of litters who studies the stars. Tonight, he delivers his soliloquy to a passer-by. A woman walking a dog. They do not know it, but it is the same canine nose that will sniff out the swollen body of the lost boy. The same voice that will murmur a verse to the weeping waves over and over.

There is no escaping the gaze of others, he tells her, *it hardens us
into something we are not.* Like the first morning, dawn approaches.
I take flight, turn for home, the safe arbour of the heronry.
I glide-glide, ash-grey body inches from that rippling mirror of images.

My communion with the city absolute, I see them all reflected there:
the murderous fox and grief-laden shells, the learned peddler of human
sadness, the breastless fever and the breathless boy forever fleeing himself,
pike-shadowed, swimming. Swimming toward a new firmament.

On the horizon, my mate's upraised bill is a steeple, a spire, a navigable
symbol of delight in a crucible of despair. He calls restlessly. I answer
with all the blessed ardour of an open-winged angel of Christ.
I have been dawned, I say, *I've been dawned.*

to never know

how much a child weighs
in the womb.
if water hurts breaking
or how long it would
have taken my uncle
to drown.
why pineapples take
so long to grow.
if people's prayers
to midnight cereus
are unanswered
cries for help.
if his eyes
were closed
or open.
if soft-shoeing blossoms
know they're dying
in the wind
at the top
of April.
if my dog knew
i was planning
to kill her.
why there are
more trees
than stars.
why starfish

don't have hearts
and ours don't
last very long.
why upturned curraghs crack
in the heat.

Jacob's Ladder

All ears and ribs, he is no bigger than a bird
on a blanket. In a Yemeni hospital, his parents
are feeding him breadcrumbs, mixed with water
and salt. He is drifting in and out of consciousness
and they are, all three, hovering the edge of
a conversation: an American on a small tv insists
that hunger is good for the gut, is a kind of favour
the body does itself. He also says lucid dreaming
is a benefit of going to bed hungry. Now, the parents
are wondering if their son's slow mouth movements
are something to be proud of. Whether beyond
his haunted eyes in need of sleep, he is dreaming
of jewelled rice or tabbouleh, or stewed lamb
on a Sunday. The mother kisses his cheek
to soothe him. The doctor lifts an eyelid
with a thumb. The ophthalmoscope shines
like a ladder up to that always-open restaurant on the Hadda
>   with the soft red tablecloths and lanterns,
>   the yoghurt and cumin and pistachio halva,
>   the families dipping bread into the same plate
>   and children playing in a leafy courtyard.
>   The sun like a juicy apricot setting behind low
>   desert hills and the child, carried home asleep
>   in his father's arms, his belly full.

Claire Loader

Claire Loader is a New Zealand born writer and photographer now living in Galway, Ireland. Her work has been published in various magazines and anthologies, including Poetry Bus, Splonk, Crannóg and Skylight47. Shortlisted for the Allingham Flash Fiction Prize in 2019, she was a winner of the Women Speak Poetry Competition in the same year and has recently been nominated for the Forward Prize.

There Are Days

when the rain falls up
and I wonder at the shape of the wind.

When I set one foot behind the other, fixated
on my toes, how bent they have become.

Days when I feel the water pooling
on my skin, settling into my pores.

There are days
when I look at my weathered hands,

see the hands of my mother, her mother –
feel the weight of all these days.

Standstill

The clock on the mantel
doesn't move, doesn't tick
doesn't measure the weight
of our skin.

We lie facing,
rescinding the minutes,
your breath a sluice,

each gasp
the only knowing
that time beats at all.

Nebulous

I hear him sometimes, the sound of his bones,
how you can hear the sea in a shell. Surprised
at the fury of something so delicate.

I hear him
like laughter behind a closed door,
like screaming underwater.

But mostly I hear him in whispers
as my eyes close to another day
of listening for words
that never come.

Telling The Bees

They say you can tell your secrets
to bees,
that they take each, one by one,
like tiny drops of pollen, dust them
into the waiting arms of a petal,
scatter them to the leas.

I watch him there day after day, talking
to the air, wonder what it is
he gifts to their wings,
my eyes fixed to the meadow,
afraid of the coming bloom.

Fallow

We toiled
the summer soughs
planted the seeds
of ourselves
watered and weeded
the earth
between us
and yet
nothing grows

The School Gate

Sometimes he says goodbye
with such ferocity, I wonder
does he know something I don't?
How he could miss me so much,
this thing that barks and rattles,
rages at the clock
we never seem to catch.
Get a move on, would ya.

Yet, there will be a time
when I am left to my own,
when he no longer demands
one more kiss, one more cuddle.
When I wish for anything to touch me
with the urgency of those small hands,
to say *I love you*
once more, before he turns.

Utility

There is gelatine in photo
paper — our lives imprinted
on congealed bones,

memory saved upon
the death of another.
One day we will be buried,

skin etched to soil,
and the worms will not
care for us.

Monochrome

I seldom reach for the box that sits
beneath my bed. My ageing hands, the dark
pigments of your broken ink.

I wish for more from these lines,
ecstasies reduced to black and white.

It does not matter
the white mould, the dusting
of a night sky upon your face —
in my heart I see you in colour.

Winter's Fruit

When evening comes I go to the orchard, tiptoe
between the wintering hedgerows, slip the fallen wall.

Silence waits upon the stone façade, the naked trees,
invisible leaves, promises of change.

It is in nesting we find hope, the dark days
of winter that offer the most. I do not care as much

for an orchard full of fruit, the luscious ripe skin of an apple,
the soft green of a pear, grass strewn with too much to carry.

Ahead lies only the decay of flesh, an end. In winter
we are always beginning.

K.T. Slattery

K.T. Slattery is a Galway based writer, originally from Memphis, Tennessee. Her work has appeared in Ropes Literary Journal, The Blue Nib, Streetcake, Planet in Peril Anthology, and various other magazines and anthologies. She received a special mention in the 2020 Desmond O'Grady Poetry Competition and was nominated for a Pushcart Prize in 2021.

I am

a platter of pork rinds mistakenly put out at the vegan
Christmas party
Marilyn sent in error to Audrey's wardrobe fitting
a young magnolia shocked when my roots touch the first
layer of blood in which they were planted
my father's muscular legs, minus their long jumping length
the clenched jaw of the Maxwells' topped off by the flare of
the James' nostrils
Olive's haunted dark interior masked with Opal's bright
smile
ten generations of stubborn female energy- sliding down the
family tree from every side to saturate and pool under my
boughs
variegated slivers of Maxwell, McCuskey, James, Gingerich,
Ketchum, and others best not mentioned, fused together by
the leaden paths I have followed, creating an ever-changing
and eccentric stained glass, configured onto an 8mm reel

If, When, How

If
I could rewrite the days
    go back
Unfold the laundry of time
    before stains
Permeated and ruined
    crisp white linens

When
A blank canvas spread
    a transparent pool
Waiting for me to dive through
    a rainbow
Leave the first spattering of colour
    a still unwritten song

How
Would I circumvent the days
    of folly
Shrill chords out of tune
    shattered glass
Disintegrated, returned to sand
    an unscathed beach

Awaiting fresh tracks

Escape to 1984

Old enough to get on my horse, head out by myself, as far as Thunder and I can get from the barn, turn, and gallop all the way back. No better feeling than holding on, splitting the air before us, creating our own vortex.

young enough to not worry about falling off

Wide-eyed enough to be curious- to bring home specimens (insects, spiders, tadpoles, even a snake) to observe, pretending I was a world-renowned scientist, everything a potential new species.

before environmental apocalypse loomed

I could be Princess Leia one moment, Indiana Jones the next- dodging imaginary poison darts as I ran through the woods. I could spin myself into Wonder Woman, then snap my fingers, twitch my nose and transform the Mississippi trees into Sherwood Forrest.

not yet labelled embarrassing/odd/annoying

A trip to Grandma's did not require seatbelts. Once I rode in the back of a pick-up truck and loved it. Heroes remained untarnished. Masks were for Halloween. Anything was still possible. Only clowns were terrifying.

back in 1984

10th of December 2020

I remember every detail of the morning-
the black 'Grumpy' bah humbug t-shirt I wore to yoga-
I even remember decorating the tree the night before.
Putting up memories collected over decades-
Uncle Scott's Naval Academy goat
Opal's painted ponies,
all the places I had been before today,
when life was safer.

I remember being at work,
the phone ringing, and the couch
I stumbled backwards onto as I
looked out the back windows seeing nothing,
but my own confusion.

I remember a day of incomprehension.
My brain said *'No.'*
A haze of ridiculous thoughts running through my head-
'I should call Dad and tell him.'
Then, the wind retreating from my lungs again-
my legs refusing to hold me.

Ten years ago,
my morning started out like any other-
no indication whatsoever you were days from
ashes and dust.

October Daisy

October daisy risen through fall hues,
last breath of summer's sparkle all alone.
From amber, orange, crimson, you breakthrough—
rising proud over leaves the wind dethroned.

November buttercup, why so delayed?
Out of place among the crackling bistre,
red and green of holly shade you in your glade,
outcast from the season of your sisters.

December daffodil, rising too soon.
Seasons melting instead of winter's snow.
Here comes cliché: you harbinger of doom.
Foreshadowing a world where nothing grows.

Ignoring your anachronistic rise.
Plastic smiles run headlong toward demise.

Immigrant

Immigrant. Refugee. Expatriate. Stranger.
Keep them all out. They all denote danger.
No turbans. No Allah. No Shiva. No heathens.
Keep them away for they all pray to demons.
My reasoning is perfect. Why yes it's quite sound.
They come to destroy us- to knock us all down.
When they come to get us, we must be prepared
So arm your young children- with hate unimpaired.
Get out your oozies and magnums and glocks
They are coming to kill us, but there it won't stop.
They treat women like vermin, no better than swine
Virtueless cowards, not like Trump... or Epstein.
Those upstanding pillars to whom we concede,
Not like them at all. They are different you see.
They're freaks. They're terrorists. Some worship the sun.
Garments stitched to hide weapons, explosives and guns.
If you won't listen to reason then examine the facts
Of the average death toll from terror attacks.
Only five less than toddlers pumped full of lead—
So close that 'golden door' before our rivers run red.
Make sure they are not welcome. Make sure they don't get in.
For the Good Lord says 'Same is virtue and different a sin.'
No more huddled masses. Keep your weary and poor.
The plaque shall be changed now to, 'Vacancies- no more.'

On the Eve of the Eve of my 39th Birthday

No, it was not a heart-attack.
Just an overfilled balloon
sitting inside my chest,
'Anxiety' written on its side
in large comic sans—
preventing the natural course of
respiration,
afraid to breathe in
lest my rib cage explode
onto the dash of
my first new car.

Terror like I have never
known, leaving me
on the side of the road,
hazards flashing
in perfect rhythm,
until my hand was
steady enough to
turn them off,
indicate,
pull back onto
the dark, lonely
road before me.

The Serenity Prayer Word Jumble

Submerged in the frustration of tides
    I cannot change.
Avoiding wild turkeys that peck and maim.
Trying to find
    the courage
to navigate the chaos on my own, to stop
looking at the Book of Decisions on the shelf,
take it down and pray I find
    serenity
in its pristine pages—
Not knowing which
    God
to ask, the one where I come from is not
open to aiding those who are not white and male.
    To know the difference
between true and false, I need all the pieces
to the puzzle, but some were soaked in tears,
the top layer flaking off, leaving a cardboard enigma,
others flushed down the toilet,
marinating in the septic tank.
I cannot change the wine in the bottle to water.
    I can
offer it to you with both hands and float away on
my inflatable raft, because I have to
    grant me,
myself,
    the

love to
> *accept the things*
that crush me will not stop
unless I have the courage to float away
> *and the wisdom to*
wear my life jacket.

Between the Last Bell of Summer and the First Bell of Fall

Too hot to do anything but swim
Sticky, suffocating, Mississippi heat
Marco
      -Polo
Marco
      -Polo
We ALL played
Before cliques
Before hormones
Marco
      Polo
Fish Out of Water!
You're it!

Though we did not want to get caught
Didn't we all really want to be Marco?
Eyes closed
Flailing about
All in the safe and secure realm
Of the shallow end

Acknowledgements

Many thanks to the editors of the following publications in which some of our poems first appeared:

Ropes – First publisher of *Immigrant* (2018)
Black Bough Poetry – First publisher of *Fallow* (2019), *Standstill* (2021) and *Monochrome* (2021)
Live Encounters - First publisher of *Girl of the Seine* as 'Annie, When I Heard' (2020)
Shot Glass Journal – First publisher of *Nebulous* (2020)
Anti Heroine Chic – First publisher of *Between the First Bell of Summer and the Last Bell of Fall* (2021)
Poetry Bus – First publisher of *Telling The Bees* (2021)
Skylight47 – First publisher of *Utility* (2021)

We would also like to give enormous thanks to Bernadette Fosberry, the fourth red pen in our little collective.

www.ingramcontent.com/pod-product-compliance
Lightning Source LLC
Chambersburg PA
CBHW020133130526
44590CB00040B/607